I0845330

Creation Creature Features
Northern Lights

For since the creation of the world God's invisible qualities—His eternal power and divine nature—have been clearly seen, being understood from what has been made, so that people are without excuse.

Romans 1:20

Wasil Science: Creation Creature Feature Series!
Northern Lights
By Joseph Wasil
Wasil Science, LLC.

From the Wasil Science Creation Creature Feature Series, Volume 57
© Copyright Wasil Science, LLC.

From the rising of the sun to the place where it sets, the name of the LORD is to be praised. The LORD is exalted over all the nations, His glory above the heavens. Who is like the LORD our God, the One who sits enthroned on high, who stoops down to look on the heavens and the earth? He raises the poor from the dust and lifts the needy from the ash heap; He seats them with princes, with the princes of His people.

Psalms 113:3-8

The Creator, the Lord Almighty, designed the incredible magnetic sphere which produces the northern lights!

Check out the northern lights!

What are the northern lights?

Energized particles originating from the sun's coronal mass ejections reach Earth's magnetic field.

When these particles interact with the atmosphere gases, they create different colored light in the sky!

The heavens declare the glory of God; the skies proclaim the work of his hands.
Day after day they pour forth speech; night after night they reveal knowledge.
Psalm 19:1-2

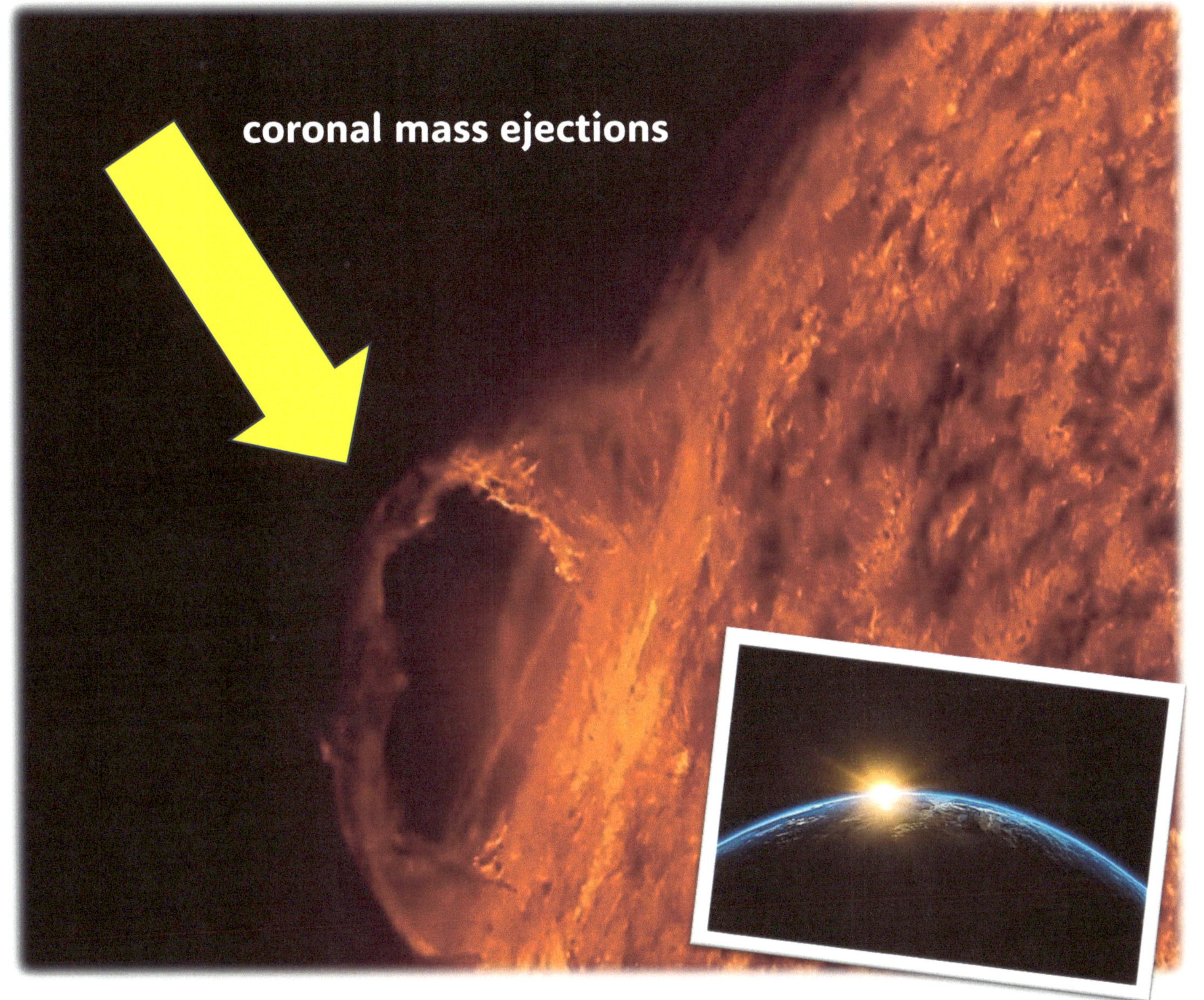

The sun is an incredible design of God and occasionally has geomagnetic storms. These often start by eruptions on the solar surface. Sunspots often experience strong magnetic activity.

Those storms that have the potential to create disturbances to Earth's magnetic field. The gas atoms release light, especially hydrogen, oxygen, and nitrogen.

These storm interactions create amazing displays of lights.

No longer will you have the
sun for light by day,
Nor for brightness will the
moon give you light;
But you will have the Lord for
an everlasting light, And your
God for your glory.
Isaiah 60:19

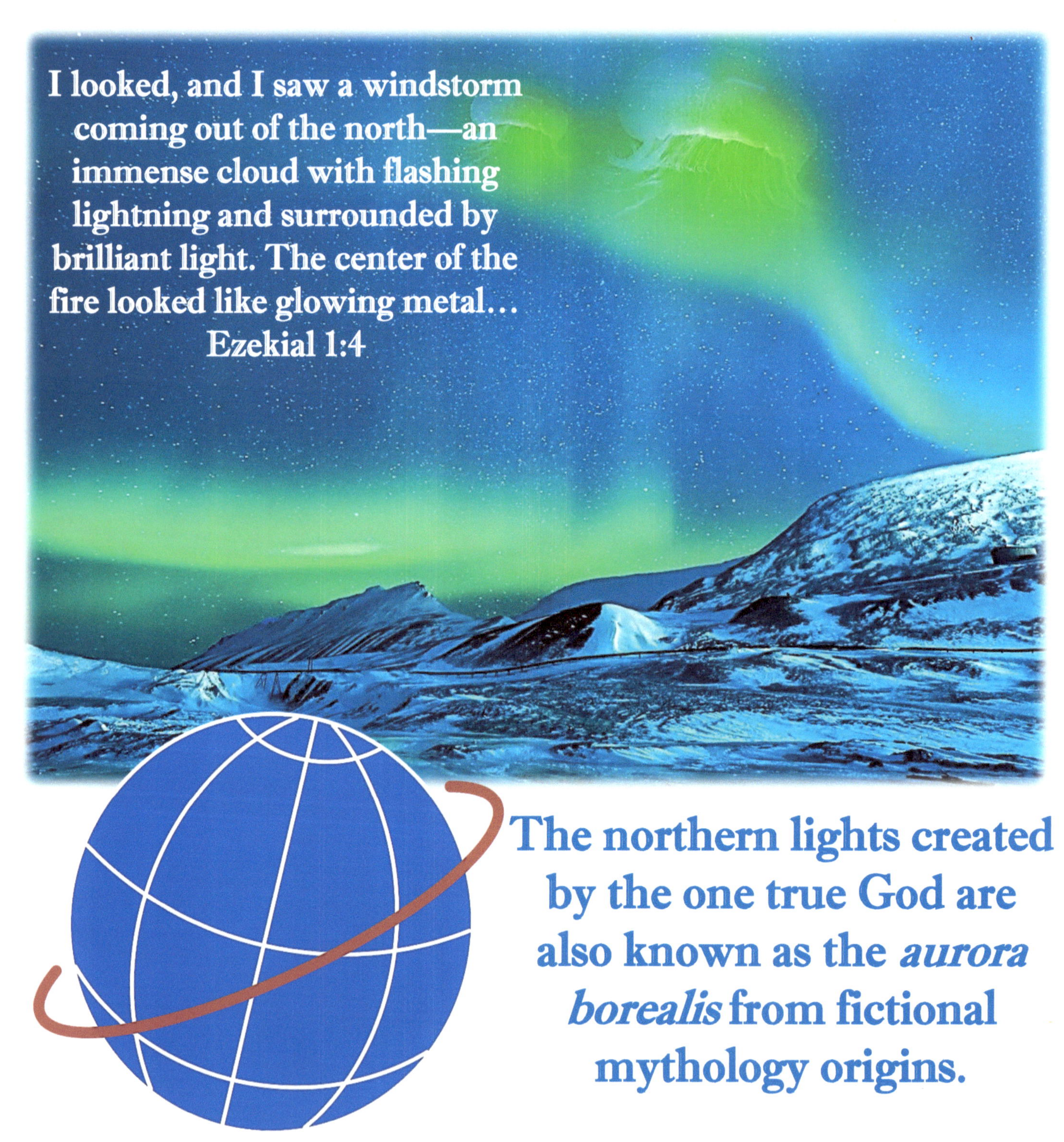

I looked, and I saw a windstorm coming out of the north—an immense cloud with flashing lightning and surrounded by brilliant light. The center of the fire looked like glowing metal…
Ezekial 1:4
The northern lights created by the one true God are also known as the *aurora borealis* from fictional mythology origins.

Galileo Galilei developed the name *aurora borealis* in 1619.

The energized particles from the sun hit the gases in Earth's upper atmosphere at speeds of up to 45 million mph!

For the sun rises with a scorching wind and withers the grass; and its flower falls off and the beauty of its appearance is destroyed; so too the rich man in the midst of his pursuits will fade away.

Most interactions that cause the northern lights appear up to 80 miles above Earth's surface and can even be seen from space!

The Finnish culture has a nickname for the northern lights.

The nickname is *revontulet,* which means fox fires. The name originates from the myth that arctic foxes were responsible for making the aurora.

God created this interaction to also happen in the southern hemisphere. These are called aurora australis, also known as the *southern lights*. From May to August is the best time to see this amazing display of God's creative power.

To Him who made the great lights,
For His lovingkindness is everlasting:
The sun to rule by day,
For His lovingkindness is everlasting…
Psalm 136:7-8

The first northern lights records were found carved into the walls of caves.

Our eyes have a difficult time detecting color at night, so the images of the northern lights often looks more colorful in photographs.

Draw & color a display of the northern lights above the mountains!

Thanks for joining us on this adventure of exploring God's incredible creation! The northern lights are amazing designs by God. Each time these incredible displays occur our Lord's incredible creation is on display. Each incredible display is created unique by our Lord Jesus!

If you have never accepted the gift of salvation let today be that day!

Romans 10:9-11

If you declare with your mouth, "Jesus is Lord," and believe in your heart that God raised Him from the dead, you will be saved. For it is with your heart that you believe and are justified, and it is with your mouth that you profess your faith and are saved. As Scripture says, "Anyone who believes in Him will never be put to shame."

We would love to hear from you!
wasil. science@gmail. com